CATHERINE DE' MEDICI
"THE BLACK QUEEN"

By Janie Havemeyer | Illustrated by Peter Malone

Series editor **Shirin Yim Bridges**
Editor **Amy Novesky**
Copy editor **Jennifer Fry**
Editorial Assistant **Ann Edwards**
Book design **Jay Mladjenovic**

Typeset in Trajan, Ringbearer, Volkswagen, and Gill Sans
Illustrations rendered in gouache

Manufactured in Singapore

Library of Congress Control Number: 2011924355

ISBN: 978-0-9834256-3-2

First Edition 10 9 8 7 6 5 4 3 2 1

Goosebottom Books LLC
710 Portofino Lane, Foster City, CA 94404

www.goosebottombooks.com

The Thinking Girl's Treasury of Dastardly Dames

CLEOPATRA
"SERPENT OF THE NILE"

AGRIPPINA
"ATROCIOUS AND FEROCIOUS"

MARY TUDOR
"BLOODY MARY"

CATHERINE DE' MEDICI
"THE BLACK QUEEN"

MARIE ANTOINETTE
"MADAME DEFICIT"

CIXI
"THE DRAGON EMPRESS"

For Olivia and Julia. ~ **Janie Havemeyer**

"The Black Queen"

One spring day in 1519, two men sat hunched over a table in Florence's enormous Palazzo Medici, casting the horoscope of Catherine, a baby born that morning. The men frowned when they were done. In the darkness of the small room, they glimpsed a calamitous event that would stain Catherine's childhood for several years. She would marry a prince who would unexpectedly inherit a throne. Catherine would give birth to future kings and queens. But what this horoscope did not foretell was that Catherine would use poison and magic to try to keep her family in power. Many would call her a schemer, a sorceress, and a snake. She would become the legendary Black Queen of France.

Paris, where Catherine spent most of her life after she became a queen.

France

Florence, where Catherine was born.

Rome, where Catherine lived for several years...

Italy

When she lived

This timeline shows when the Dastardly Dames were born.

69 BC	15 AD		1516 AD	1519 AD		1755 AD	1835 AD
Cleopatra	Agrippina		Mary Tudor	Catherine de' Medici		Marie Antoinette	Cixi

HER STORY

Catherine de' Medici was born on April 13, 1519, into the powerful Medici family, who had helped rule Florence, Italy, for generations. When Catherine was born, both her parents were very sick, and they only lived a few weeks after her birth. Catherine grew up with her grandmother, her aunt, and her cousins on the lush grounds of the Medici Palace. She was called the Duchessina, since her father, Lorenzo, had been a duke.

One of Catherine's most powerful relatives was Pope Clement VII, her great-uncle, who lived many miles away in the city of Rome. Clement was always plotting and scheming to add to his family's power and wealth and he had big plans for Catherine. As he sat upon his throne, corpulent Clement dreamed of all the important men he might befriend by arranging a marriage to his niece Catherine.

But before he could plan anything, an army of angry rebels plundered and burned Rome. Clement escaped to his fortress along the Tiber River. When news of the destruction spread, the Pope and all his Medici relatives were blamed. Angry Florentines drove the Medici out of Florence but decided to keep eight-year-old Catherine as a hostage. The new rulers of Florence locked her up in a convent cell and debated her fate. Some men voted to kill her. But others decided Catherine was more valuable alive. Catherine prayed that she would survive. It took three years for the Pope to regain control of Florence and set Catherine free. Afterwards, Clement brought her to Rome to live with him.

A portrait of Catherine's great-uncle, Pope Clement VII, painted by Sebastiano del Piombo around 1530.

You can still visit the Castel d'Angelo in Rome. This is where Clement barricaded himself against the rebels.

This painting by Jacopo Chimenti (1551-1640), depicting Catherine and Henry's marriage ceremony, now hangs in the Uffizi Gallery next to the Medici Palace in Florence. Chimenti flatteringly painted Catherine as slim and tall!

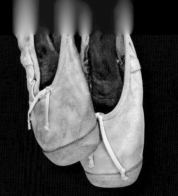

Catherine was now eleven, almost old enough for marriage. The French king wanted to add more Italian territories to his empire. Maybe Clement could make a deal with him—land in exchange for Catherine's marriage into the French royal family. It was an ambitious plan since Catherine was a commoner, but King Francis was greedy too, so he agreed.

Catherine smiled when she saw her betrothed's portrait. He was tall and handsome, a great catch for a short, plain girl like her. She set to work ordering gowns glittering with jewels and packing chests with pearls, golden belts, and rings. She intended to make a dazzling first impression.

In the fall, Catherine married Prince Henry, Duke of Orleans, the second son of King Francis. They were both fourteen. After weeks of banquets, masked balls, and concerts, Catherine rode back with the Royal Court to her new home in Paris. She sat up straight on her black stallion, ignoring the whispers that she was only a merchant's daughter. Her unusual way of riding sitting sideways on her horse was the first of many innovations she introduced to France.

What she brought to France

If it were not for Catherine, the French may not have the side saddle, the high heeled shoe, forks for eating, the folding fan, the ladies' handkerchief, the violin, modern ballet and opera, and the custom of wearing underpants under one's clothes. Before the pantaloon, French men could see up ladies' skirts when they mounted their horses!

Henry and Catherine were married when they were fourteen, which was common at that time. She adored him for the rest of her life.

But at court, things did not turn out as Catherine had hoped. The prince ignored her, the French treated her like an outsider, and worst of all, her husband was in love with the beautiful Diane de Poitiers.

Catherine turned to the Italian courtiers she had brought with her to France for help. Her cobbler made new shoes with two-inch heels so Catherine was now more than five feet tall. Her perfumer made her seductive scents to wear. The French had never used perfume before. Her astronomer consulted the stars to predict Catherine's future. Some whispered that he dabbled in black magic for the princess, casting spells and mixing love potions. Pretty soon, the French court began to admire Catherine's unique style, although Henry still barely noticed his wife.

Diane de Poitiers, King Henry's mistress. She was closely linked to the family, whether Catherine liked it or not, as the king had her supervise the

Some say that King Henry's cipher, displayed in many of his buildings, was a tribute to his love for Diane, combining an H for Henry and a D for Diane. Other scholars say that it is a C for Catherine, not a D. Still others say that all three letters are shown, representing the complicated relationship between Catherine, Henry, and Diane.

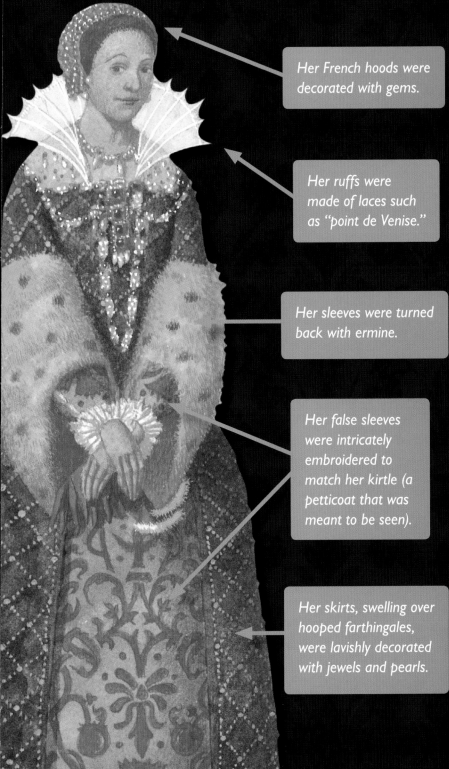

Her French hoods were decorated with gems.

Her ruffs were made of laces such as "point de Venise."

Her sleeves were turned back with ermine.

Her false sleeves were intricately embroidered to match her kirtle (a petticoat that was meant to be seen).

Her skirts, swelling over hooped farthingales, were lavishly decorated with jewels and pearls.

What she wore

Catherine was almost five feet tall. She had pale brown hair, olive skin, a large nose, and eyes that bulged. Her big eyes were a common trait of the Medici family. No one called her attractive but she made up for that by dressing very well, and wearing makeup and perfume. Her gowns made it very clear that she came from one of the wealthiest families in Europe. Later in her life she lightened her hair with bleach since blond hair was supposed to be the most attractive hair color in the French court.

Then Francis, Henry's older brother and heir to the throne, developed a high fever and died. Along the twisting corridors of the Chateau de Chaumont, the whispering began. Was he poisoned? Fingers pointed at Catherine. In the first place, she was from Florence and Italians had a reputation for poisoning people. In the second, her husband was now heir to the throne. Now, Catherine would one day be queen.

All the nasty gossip swirling around Catherine had damaged her hard-earned reputation. She was now as unpopular as the sewer rats. To make matters worse, the couple had no children to inherit the crown. Catherine knew that she had to produce a son if she wanted to earn her way back into favor and win her husband's affection.

Whom she bore

Francis II of France, born 1544, died 1560. King from 1559.

Elizabeth of Valois, born 1545, died 1568. Queen of Spain from 1559.

Claude of Valois, born 1547, died 1575. Duchess of Lorraine from 1559.

Charles IX of France, born 1550, died 1574. King from 1560.

When Henry was crowned King Henry II eleven years later, Catherine had done her duty by not only giving birth to an heir, Francis, who would inherit the throne, but also to baby Louis and daughters Elizabeth and Claude. Catherine could breathe a sigh of relief. Her Medici-blooded family would continue to rule France. Henry was happy too.

Queen Catherine stood proudly in her high-heeled shoes. She now straddled her horse like a man and carried a crossbow when she rode. Trumpets announced her arrival at important events. Diane de Poitiers was still the king's favorite, but now Henry spent time with Catherine and even put her in charge when he left the country to fight. She loved him. He respected her. Once again, the French were grateful to Catherine when she gave birth to three more sons and three more daughters, although three of the babies, including Louis, died.

Henry III of France, born 1551, died 1589. King from 1574.

Margaret of Valois, commonly called Margot, born 1553, died 1615. Queen of Navarre from 1572, and of France from 1589.

Francis, Duke of Anjou and Alençon, born 1555, died 1584.

Catherine's three babies who did not survive infancy: Louis, Victoria, and Joan of Valois.

Then, one night Catherine dreamed that Henry lay on the ground covered in blood. That afternoon, Henry had a terrible accident while jousting. His opponent's lance struck his helmet and a wood splinter pierced his eye.

Catherine stood beside Henry's bed for days until he died. Although he had never loved her, she adored him. In the privacy of her bedroom she wept. But in her despair, Catherine remembered how powerless she felt locked away in Florentine convents. She knew she couldn't waste a minute more grieving. She needed to take action because her family's future was at stake.

This painting, opposite, shows the fatal joust of Henry II. During the joust, Henry was struck in the helmet by the lance of his opponent. Splinters went through the helmet and into his eye, and possibly through it into his brain. He lived for eleven days before passing away. The infamous Nostradamus, one of Catherine's advisors, reportedly predicted this tragic event in a poem:

©THoog/Creative Commons 2.0

The young lion will overcome the older one,
On the field of combat in a single battle;
He will pierce his eyes through a golden cage,
Two wounds made one, then he dies a cruel death.

But she was too late. In the ten days that Henry had been hovering between life and death, the powerful Guise family had taken control. Catherine's teenaged son, Francis, would be king in name only and the Guise brothers would make all the major decisions. Catherine was furious. She studied her astrological charts to predict the future. Some even say that she gazed into her astronomer's magic mirror to see how many years her sons would rule France. According to legend, what she saw disturbed her, especially when the last face to appear was not one of her sons. Catherine realized she would have to be clever and cunning to protect her children.

Did Catherine see the face of Henry of Navarre in her magic mirror? Although three of her sons would become king, all died without sons to inherit the throne. The French crown passed out of Catherine's immediate family to her son in law, Henry of Navarre.

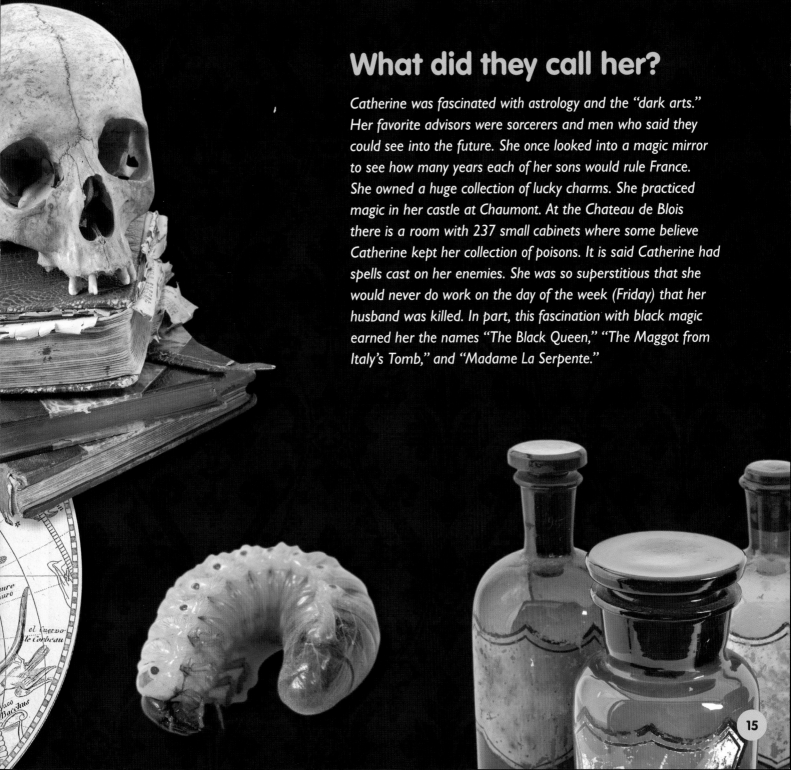

What did they call her?

Catherine was fascinated with astrology and the "dark arts." Her favorite advisors were sorcerers and men who said they could see into the future. She once looked into a magic mirror to see how many years each of her sons would rule France. She owned a huge collection of lucky charms. She practiced magic in her castle at Chaumont. At the Chateau de Blois there is a room with 237 small cabinets where some believe Catherine kept her collection of poisons. It is said Catherine had spells cast on her enemies. She was so superstitious that she would never do work on the day of the week (Friday) that her husband was killed. In part, this fascination with black magic earned her the names "The Black Queen," "The Maggot from Italy's Tomb," and "Madame La Serpente."

Catherine's court

Catherine believed that no matter how bad things were, an amazing show always helped. She invited hundreds of beautiful women to her court and called them her "Flying Squadron." They dressed like goddesses in silk and gold and wore wooden corsets to create thirteen-inch waists. Catherine organized ballets, jousts, and mock battles. Her court festivals were so fantastic that you might see a floating fortress, elaborately decorated barges, chariots pulled by sea horses, and huge artificial whales and tortoises. Catherine wanted to show the world that her kingdom was the most glorious.

As the mirror had predicted, Francis II was king for less than two years. He died from an ear infection. When Catherine heard the news, she knew she had to act first and grieve later. She rushed to block all the entrances to her castle and called a special meeting. Her ten-year-old son, Charles, was too young to be crowned King of France. "I have decided to govern the state, as a devoted mother must do!" Catherine declared. She had a regal seal made for her that said Governor of the Kingdom.

Catherine was in charge at last! She was forty-one. She was no longer the eager bride of a prince, but a plump monarch who dressed in black dresses, veils, and capes. She stood out like a vulture among the peacocks in her court. She had important things to do. She needed to preserve her family's power and to arrange royal marriages for all her children. If she succeeded, her descendants might rule Europe one day. This became one of her greatest ambitions.

LÉGENDE DU DESSIN ORIGINAL.

s tyrans insensez n'estants iamais contents,
uentent tous les iours autres nouueaux torments,
leur ardant courroux ne suffit nulle paine:
z s'esgaient à voir souffrir cruelle mort.
ux pauures innocents, qu'ilz font mourir à tort,
Mo—rant par tel tourments leur tant mortelle haine.

G   Dv

18

But Catherine's real struggles were just beginning. France was on the verge of civil war. For centuries, the French had been followers of the Catholic religion. During her husband's reign, a growing number of citizens became followers of a new religion called Protestantism. They were called Huguenots. The Catholic nobility felt threatened by the Huguenots and forbade them to practice their religion in France.

Pretty soon, the first of eight wars erupted between Catholics and Huguenots. Both groups tried to outdo each other in wicked acts of revenge. Huguenots slashed the throats of Catholic monks. Catholic soldiers drowned and beheaded Huguenots. Rebels even stole King Francis' heart from an urn in Paris and burned it. The queen was so mad she decided to punish the man who wounded her husband in the joust. She had never forgiven him. She ordered her men to capture, behead, and quarter him. Many began to believe that Catherine would do anything to get rid of her enemies—hire assassins, cast spells, and send poisoned apples and gloves to her victims. Some even said she ate little children!

By now Catherine was getting used to all the horrible stories about her, especially as some of them were true.

A miniature painting of Margot and Henry of Navarre, originally painted as an illumination for one of Catherine's prayer books.

20

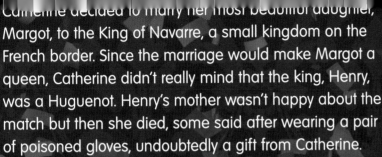

Catherine decided to marry her most beautiful daughter, Margot, to the King of Navarre, a small kingdom on the French border. Since the marriage would make Margot a queen, Catherine didn't really mind that the king, Henry, was a Huguenot. Henry's mother wasn't happy about the match but then she died, some said after wearing a pair of poisoned gloves, undoubtedly a gift from Catherine.

As Margot and Henry's wedding day approached, strangers from around the country flocked to Paris to take part in the wedding festivities. Beggars and prostitutes pressed up against peasants and nobles. Tension ran high over a royal match between a Catholic and a Protestant.

But back at her castle, the queen was plotting her most dastardly act. Catherine knew her political rival, the Huguenot Admiral Coligny, would be coming to the wedding, so she set a trap. She hired an assassin to kill him. But on the designated morning, the assassin misfired. The admiral was wounded but not killed. Hearing the dreadful news, Catherine realized her family's fate hung in the balance. If the Huguenots discovered who had tried to kill their commander, they would surely launch an attack. With not a minute to spare, Catherine set a new plan in motion, one that would give birth to the legend of the Black Queen of France.

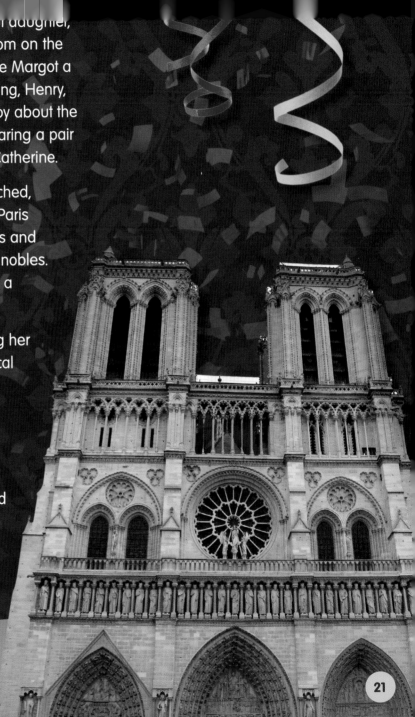

Two days later, in the pre-dawn hours of the feast day of Saint Bartholomew, the king's bodyguards and troops barged into the admiral's hotel, stabbing him in the chest and throwing his body out of the window. Another troop of royal guards stormed into the palace, slashing the throats of Catherine's Huguenot guests while they slept. Catherine hid in her bedroom listening to the screams of terror, audible proof her dastardly plan had worked. By dawn, most of the senior Huguenots were dead.

Now, murder moved into the streets of the capital. Royal troops and Catholics stirred up by the massacre attacked any Huguenot they could find. Anyone wearing the distinctive black and white clothes of a Huguenot was stabbed, beaten, and mutilated. By the afternoon, an angry mob had taken over Paris. Coligny's corpse was cut into pieces and hurled into the Seine River. Neighbors robbed neighbors. Old enemies sought revenge. Madness spread like wildfire throughout the kingdom. For weeks, Catholics and Huguenots continued to kill each other.

Catherine was blamed for the nationwide killing spree. She had killed the Huguenot leaders but she had lost control of her country to angry mobs. Thousands died throughout her kingdom. Catherine's reputation was stained forever. But the queen was relieved. Her family was still in charge and Coligny was dead. She sent a gift to the Pope to celebrate. When he opened it, the embalmed head of their enemy Coligny stared back at him.

This painting shows Admiral Coligny's body being thrown out of a window after the second—this time successful—assassination attempt.

The Huguenot leader, Gaspard de Coligny.

This painting shows Queen Catherine surveying the bodies of dead Huguenots after the massacre. The artist, Edouard Debat-Ponsan, attached some text to his painting, stating that many Huguenots were killed that day.

By the time Charles IX died of tuberculosis and his brother Henry became king, Catherine was one of the most hated women in France. Even her daughter Margot hated her. Catherine was getting old and fat. Her bones and muscles ached. She had terrible toothaches. But she was as determined as ever to preserve her family's dynasty. Two of her sons were still alive. Neither of them had children. But Catherine had high hopes for the future. After all, her favorite son was now king.

King Henry was a man who liked to curl his hair, try on women's clothes, and spray himself with perfume. He spent most of his days riding through the forest and partying while war broke out in France. Henry was just as unpopular as his mother and over time he blamed her for all his problems. Soon, he began to trust no one, imagining assassins around every corner. He was so paranoid that he had his clothes embroidered with skulls.

A contemporary portrait showing the new King of France with his mother.

What she ate

Catherine's appetite was supposed to be enormous and sometimes she ate so much she made herself sick. Gossip spread that as Catherine got fatter, she often rode her horses to death. Her favorite dish was called cibreo, a Florentine stew of gizzards, testicles, offal, and cockerels' coxcombs (the fleshy comb on the top of a chicken).

King Henry was going insane and about to lose his kingdom. Then, Catherine's youngest son, Francois, died of tuberculosis. For the first time in her life, Catherine felt like giving up. She remembered the premonition in the magic mirror and now understood why a new face had appeared after her son Henry. Her family's reign was coming to an end.

One day, Henry announced that his mother was no longer in charge of anything. "I have been a valet for too long!" he shouted. Catherine was heartbroken. She had fought so hard to preserve her family's crown. She had never expected the son she had spoiled to treat her so cruelly. Catherine spent most of her days in bed praying for Henry. The only comfort she felt was looking at her most cherished possession, the portrait of her one true love, King Henry II.

Comfort in her loneliness

Catherine loved animals, especially dogs and birds. She kept a royal menagerie of lions and bears that lumbered behind her as she paraded from castle to castle. A long-tailed monkey and a green parrot were some of her pets. She loved to collect things and had seven stuffed alligators hanging in her study in the Hotel de la Reine palace.

On a cold winter afternoon in 1589, sixty-nine-year-old Catherine de' Medici died. When the herbs used to embalm her body did not work and her corpse started to smell, Henry buried her in a churchyard in the city of Blois. She would not lie next to her husband in the Parisian chapel she had built for them both (although she was eventually moved there twenty-one years later). The short, plain teenager who had arrived in France fifty-five years earlier was buried like a pauper in an unmarked grave. Catherine, devoted mother and fearless ruler, was gone, but her legend would live on. Catherine de' Medici would forever be remembered as the evil Black Queen of France.